1

ART SCHOOL

From teaching.

Graeme Smith

PUBLISHED ON AMAZON.com
by
LABYRINTH BOOKS

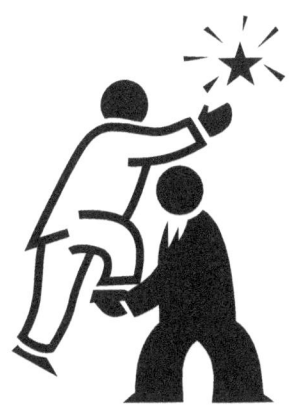

DEDICATION:

This book is dedicated to my family.
Hele-ly (Ly).
       my wife:

Ingrid.
       our daughter:

Marie.
       my former wife:

Fiona, Natalie and Michael
       our children:

Georgie
       Michael's wife:

Pearl, Kiki and Martha.
       their children:

They have had to put up with me for many years and I thank them for that.
I hope this book gives them an insight into what has occupied me much of the time.
They have all achieved worthwhile and interesting careers in the absence of much help from me.
I congratulate them for their achievements.

THANKS:

I greatly appreciate the contribution made to this book by comments and suggestions from:

Mike Barr – Adelaide, Australia

Richard Bruland - Los Angeles, USA

Tracey Creighton - Merimbula, Australia

Evelyn Dunphy – Maine, USA

Geoff Fellows – Wagga Wagga, Australia

Michelle Grace - Brisbane, Australia

Leanne Halls – North Sydney, Australia

Heidi Jeffries – Ferny Hills, Australia

Kathy Kay Voysey - Mudgee, Australia.

Vince Miller – publisher:

('Australian Artist' and 'International Artist)

John Newell - Ontario, Canada

David Voigt – Yarramalong, Australia.

Acknowledgement:

John Hill, West Sussex, United Kingdom assisted with the original proof reading.

Many of his comments on the manuscript were incorporated in this book.

I am very grateful to John for his help.

John and Sakura's website is www.johnhillwatercolour.com

HOW TO USE THIS BOOK.

First think - then do.
Usually people don't think through things to the level they need to.
Because of that, they have projects instead of tasks on their "to do" list.
That leads to procrastination as it hasn't been broken down to a task level.

So go through your book once to understand it.
Go through it again.

Then start at the idea you would like to implement first.
Make notes of the steps you will need to take and the resources required.
Use these notes to create a step by step system for implementing the guide.
Often you will not refer back to an original, as you've created YOUR system.

The first question you ask and answer is "Why is this being done?"
How does this align with where you want to get to?
What are the strategic implications of doing this?
Does this fit with getting to a goal in the shortest and fastest amount of time?

What would it be like if it were totally successful?
Define it - what is success for this project and how will you know?

Now brainstorm all the tasks that are involved in your project.
It's important not to go linear too fast with this.
By linear, I mean step one, step two, step three, and step four.
You end up cutting off options.
Plan step one, two, and three, a specific step that might be number four.
If you start steps quickly, other ways of one, two or three may not appear.

The first third of any brainstorming session is really easy.
Just come up with lots of ideas.
The second third is challenging - go through ideas and see where they lead.
Then push yourself to think a little bit outside the box.
That's often where the big idea is!

That's where the most powerful way to get a project done fastest - is.
Most people never get to that level and end up short-changing themselves.
Then their project takes longer and they also procrastinate.
This final brainstorming part of the equation is incredibly important.

Once you fully brainstorm put your options into a linear sequence.
Then you can figure out what you've overlooked.
Everything becomes obvious as you get your tasks in order.
Now add missing steps and you have laid out your task list for this project.

Once you've organized the tasks into a linear process decide:
What things can you start immediately?
What can be started that is not dependent on things to occur before them?
Obviously that is step one.
Step five or six or twenty that don't really rely on anything else to get done.
You can get started on them right away too.

Now use a folder.
Write things you think of at the time and also cross off things as you do them.
Add in stuff that is relevant from time to time.

WHAT IS MARKETING?

Marketing is the process of finding buyers AND making sales
It is exactly the same process no matter what is being sold!
Sometimes the process is simple such as selling apples at a roadside stall.
In other cases it is very complex.
Selling aero-planes for a government's air-force would be an example of that.
Most, including selling artworks, is somewhere in between these poles.

Think about fishing and you'll understand marketing.
Does a fisherman catch anything out in a desert?
NO, for there are simply no fish there.

You must market where there are possible buyers.
A fisherman must go where the fish are – where there is water.
That's a start but there are still no fish in a swimming pool are there?
They need to be in the right kind of water – a river, lake or at sea.

But different fish swim in different waters!
Sharks and marlin are in the ocean, while bream live mainly in rivers.
Likewise you must know who you are targeting with your marketing.
Will it be businesses, first home buyers, investors or what?
Each will need a different marketing program.
OK you are now in the right water for the kind of fish you are after!
Are you there at the right time?

Some species are nocturnal and they are not caught during the day.
So your marketing needs to be when the target is likely to be most receptive.
Will it be at work, nights or weekends?

You are at the right place and time so what do you use to catch a fish?
Usually you'll have a fishing rod.
Is it the right kind for the fish you want to catch?
You won't catch a shark with the kind of rod that takes a trout!
Your marketing must be attractive to the people you are after.

Do you have the right bait?
Again different bait attracts different fish.
A carcass for the shark but just a worm for many other species.
Can you provide something that your target market will find attractive?

But throwing any bait into the water catches nothing at all!
The bait must be attached to a hook.
Without the fish taking the hook there is no catch.
Different hooks are needed for different kinds of fish.

Different hooks are also needed for different markets.
The hook that will get your market to take the next step towards a purchase
is the right hook.
But this only needs to be a little step.

But hooks only catch the fish.
They are in the water, not on you boat or beach so attach the hook to a line.
What is your line like?
Is it strong enough you the fish you are after?
Again this varies for the kind of fish.

How do you get a prospect to seriously consider what you are seeking?
For someone buying a print it will not need to be sophisticated.
But selling an original Renoir will be considerably more complicated.

That doesn't bring in a fish the line needs a reel for that to happen.
Again different reels for different fish.
The right reel allows you to bring the fish to the end of your fishing line.
But it's still not in the boat is it?

You need to lift the fish out of the water into your boat or onto a beach.
Fishing nets do this.
But now you have your catch.
The fish is yours to do what you want with.

You can even sell the fish!

But who might want to buy?

It could be someone sells the fish either as food or live for a fish-tank or pool.

They could even be for re-stocking natural water places.

Where can you find them?

You must look where the fish buyers are!

Follow the path of the fisherman.

And eventually you have a prospect asking can they buy.

You have made a sale **AND** you can make more sales the same way.

OK how do you make the sale?

There are five key groups.

So it's a five step process.

In order you work from the top through to the bottom group.

SUSPECTS are people who might possibly want what you have for sale.

PROSPECTS are people likely to want what you have for sale.

BUYERS are those who have bought what you are selling.

REPEAT BUYERS continue to buy what you sell.

ADVOCATES help you sell to others.

The reverse sequence is the order of importance to your sales.

INDEX: WORKSHOPS.

Chapter One: Organize a workshop.

1. Setting up demonstrations and/or workshops

Lots of artists provide classes, demonstrations or workshops.
To supplement art income, test ideas on other people, or help fellow artists.
You can even make quite a good income from this sort of activity.

Write six reasons why you'd like to run a workshop or a demonstration.
Underline the most important of them.
There must be a reason; otherwise there's no point in the exercise.
Now you know why you are going to demonstrate or run a workshop,
It could easily be different from any I have indicated, or even several of them,

Are you offering your services to make money?
There's nothing wrong with that.
No point if an approach you plan to use means no money, or not enough.
Do you know things that most don't, and want to share this with people?
Will it help further your career?

Make certain you set it up to do just that!
Say you are running demonstrations as a way of making money,
But as a way of meeting people, the same set up could be perfectly fine.
In other words plan what you do or you may not achieve your goals.
If you provide people with value for money, almost any goal can be achieved.

Who can help your project actually happen?
What organizations run classes, demonstrations or workshops?
There are art societies and similar groups of artists.
They are the most common groups who run courses or workshops for artists.

Educational institutions conduct demonstrations and workshops.
This is particularly so if they're involved in adult education,
Although more often they run classes.
The classes are either for their students, or the general community.

There are also special artists' holiday accommodation venues.
They conduct workshops or classes on a regular basis.
Sometimes galleries do this too, although usually they'll use their own artists.

O.K. now you've planned a suitable demonstration or workshop.
Write it all down.
Read through it from the point of view of someone attending your course.
Have you covered everything they'd want to know?
For example will it be practical?
Who supplies the materials, if it is?
If it's the student, what do they need to bring?

Double-check everything.
Then write it out in several different ways.
Why several different ways, you may ask?
Well each different way will tend to suggest some new ideas for you to use.
Different approaches for educational institutions compared to art societies.

Many students may be the same, but the organizations are different.
They operate in different ways, which you need to take into account.
Educational institutions usually collect money at enrollment for all courses.
Art societies collect money from members for a course often not in advance.
But each tends to use different language too.

The next thing you need to do is plan a marketing campaign.
No, not to get people to come to your demonstration or workshop!
It will be to sell your proposal to the group concerned.

Approach any group initially to let them know you are available.
It would be a good idea if you also can tell them what you could do.

Who do you need to contact?
When is the best time?
It may be late in the year for next year, or a month or so ahead of time.

What sort of workshops do they usually run?
Is yours a fit or different?
What is your background?
Why should they use you?
What can you do for them?

The last one is the really important one.
Once you have all this worked out it's time to approach the different groups.
Naturally you'll need different approaches for each.

Well, they have your proposal and are interested, what next?
Follow up, that's what!
Ask when they will have decided what to do.
Give them a ring at about that time, or a little sooner.
Find out how things are going (and so they don't forget your proposal).

Let's say they don't go ahead with your great workshop.
Find out what the problem was but do this politely.
Are they short of money right now, or not having any more courses like this?
There could be any number of other reasons too.

This information will help you prepare a better proposal next time.
So re-work your ideas and present them again at an appropriate time.
Maintain contact to find out about other workshop ideas they're interested in.
They could be ones you also can do.

Of course you can organize things yourself.
Then you should earn more as obviously there's more to do.
In this case you'll also need considerably more organizing skills.

2. Setting up and doing your own demonstrations!

Why do you want to do this?
Are you trying to make money?
Do you want to boost your ego?
Would you like to help people?
Have people asked you?
Perhaps you've done it before?
You promote existing classes and attract new students (John Hill UK).

What exactly are you going to do?
Why will people want to see this demonstration?
Have you practiced sufficiently?
How long does it take?
Can the time taken vary?
Will you need to supply notes or other handouts?

How are you going to do it?
Who will want to attend?
How are you going to reach the people who should attend?
Have they seen something like your demonstration before?
What will attract them to your course?
Where will you find the people who would like your demonstration?

How much should you charge?
What will it cost you?
How much do you want to make?
How many people do you need there?
What is the most you can handle?
What is the smallest attendance you need to still make money?
What will it cost them (there may be costs above your charge)?

When will this happen?
What time of the year is best?
What day of the week and what time is best?

Where would be a good place?
Can you obtain such a place?
What (part of your) town, city, suburb, area would be best?
What exactly do you need?
Are you flexible?

Who will you need there to help you?
Who will you need to contact about the demonstration?
How will they know?

Sit down and think for a while.
Read the questions, as well as others that come to mind (write them down).
Write down answers to all the questions (including your other ones).

See how they fit together.
Make sure you test answers against reasons for doing the demonstration,
Otherwise the whole idea is a waste of time.
You should have planned a suitable demonstration and written it all down.
Still shuffle ideas around so they are in a more sensible order than at first.

Read through from the point of view of someone attending your course.
Make sure it's the kind of person you want to attract.
Have you covered everything they'd want to know?
Double-check everything and then write it out in several different ways.
Each different way will tend to suggest some new ideas for you to use.

The next thing to do is plan a marketing campaign.

You need to get people to come to your demonstration.
Who do you need to contact?
When is the best time?
How will you do it?
What is your background?
Why should artists come to your demonstration?
What can you do for them?

Can you do it?

Best of luck, for it is fun and you can make money.

Actually sit down and answer the questions asked.

Which means you'll then know whether you can do this and how.

3. How could you actually organize a workshop?

Here's an outline of a possible workshop.
Using recognised and experienced artists and teachers

Your students
Generally hobby and semi-professional artists.
Occasionally professional artists.

The format
Week-end (2 days)
Lunch & morning/afternoon tea each day.
No enrollment after (close date)
No extra materials to be bought.
Maximum might be 15 whilst the minimum is the break/even number.
Do things regularly e.g. at Easter, Xmas, end of financial year, etc.
Include a research component so YOU learn something each time.

Provide incentives:
Free report for early bird enrollers.
Extra discount for special groups (you decide).
Leverage schools, magazines, art societies and other groups.
Sell before course at reduced price. (e.g. At this course pay for the next one.)
Up-sell future courses (block of 4 for price of 3)
Add-ons - art materials
Cross-sell reports, tapes, videos, artist's prints, art supplies, etc.

Don't forget to follow up:
Questionnaire after course.
Mailing list now for future so can sidestep societies, schools, etc.

What about the money?
See earlier elsewhere.

What does a teacher receive (you or someone else)?
Stress importance of actual teaching ability as well as artistic ability.

Standard artist teacher payment
For all courses.
$500 (or whatever) for artist (flat fee any number of students to 15)
No other fee, no expenses
You pay all expenses
They stay with you if contra deal not organized

Artist teacher supplies
'My Story' which is their own story.
Course notes and materials needed with alternatives
Who would benefit from their course?
Commonsense advice
Professional tuition
Practical help or whatever.

What you need to do (even if you are not the teacher)?
Develop mailing lists.
Need high school, art societies, art teachers and artists as attendees.

Write and print literature.
Headings are **MOST** important
Focus on factors that qualify the potentlal student (sort them out).

Pre-enrollment literature designed to contact those who'd benefit most.
Focus on what's in it for them, which are the benefits.
Be specific ... which means that .. (key benefits).
Emphasize value factors. (training, skill, commitment, status, their investment, testimonials.

Say how you'll meet their needs.
Use photographs and cartoons

State offer

Assume everyone is interested and will come.

Call for action

Tell people what to do.

After-sales literature

Similar to pre-sales literature

Help student explain course to others, answer questions, add to knowledge.

Double check everything to make sure this is what you do.

4. Can you under-promise but over-deliver?

The secret of student satisfaction is to deliver more than they expect.
If students expect little and you deliver more then you have 'over-delivered'.
Your student won't just be satisfied, but delighted.
All that is required is that you plan ahead.

The more you can delight your students, the happier they will be.
AND the more they will come back for repeat doses.
These days, when sales are difficult such strategies may even be essential.
Times like this well-prepared teachers take advantage of opportunities.
They are opportunities missed by those who may not be as well prepared.
Gain market share and student loyalty during a down turn.
This tends to be longer lasting and stronger than if gained in boom times.

Overwhelm your customers with personal and unexpected service.
That's the single best way to keep them for life.
Provided you are dedicated to delivering exactly what the student wants.

Rash promises should be avoided.
Hype only creates suspicion particularly when the reality is different.
It's better to promise little.
Only say or do enough to get your client to sample your teaching.
In fact it's a strategy that sets up enhanced satisfaction by your clients.

Investigate how little you need to promise someone.
So they enroll in one of your classes.

But nothing will ever happen unless you do something.
In other words to see ANY results you have to take ACTION.
And a great way to make sure you do this is to create an action plan.
Once you know what you need to take action on, it's much easier to **DO** it.

You are excited about stuff you have discovered and tried from a book.
You'll probably want to implement them all.

Well you shouldn't! for it's CRITICAL that you NARROW your focus.
So decide on three main goals you want to achieve with your workshop.
Look for 3 key areas where you take action immediately with your teaching.
Then you'll have a much clearer idea what you need to do.
You don't have to do everything all at once … or ever!
Implementing 1 or 2 of the most basic strategies can bring amazing results.

Focus on implementing only a few strategies at a time.
Take **ACTION**, and almost always you'll be able to report incredible results!
Do you keep a record of your action plans and how they turn out?
Use an ordinary notebook and be surprised as you realize what happens.

5. Could you run a course from someone else's material?

Most courses are like this.
You could use my An Art Program as a basis.
Begin with Learn to Copy.
Then there is a curriculum that you teach from.
Naturally when you run your own courses things are different.

Decide what you will cover.
Will it be a single course or a series of course?
Your courses will be local unless you are running an eCourse.

Start small.
Do not have many students (maybe 5).
Do not be ambitious in what you will cover.
Do not charge a high fee.
The main aim is to get started and learn what happens.

Your second course should build on the first one.
Fix anything that you were unhappy with.
Still keep the course small and cheap.
That means you repeat courses for new students.

As you run more courses slowly build the number of students.
Slowly build up the fee charged as you get better.
You can then increase the time you spend and earn more that way.

Target anyone to start with.
There's no-one who cannot use your course!
Down the track you might specialize in artists but it might not be necessary.

Once you are confident with your course.
Then consider adding another course with a different focus.
This could still be linked to your original course.
How to stretch watercolour paper to follow the water-colour wash course.

Early students can return to this one.

Eventually you might have a series of courses.

Income increases with more courses, more students and higher fees.

But first ones must be right.

Take no chances.

Chapter Two: A school is the next step.

1. Could you establish a school?
2. Another set of initials!
3. Do you have a procedures manual?
4. How do you delegate?
5. A sample Job Description for an art teacher.

1. Could you establish a school?

You have conducted many lessons.
Lessons are usually short (1 or 2 hours) and one-off.
They focus on a single subject by one teacher.

A course is also a one-off on a single subject.
But it covers a number of lessons (3 to 10).
There could be multiple teachers too.

Workshops are one-off but over longer time span.
They might go from ½ day to several days.
Again there could be multiple teachers.

The next thing is a school.
A school generally has multiple courses and a number of teachers.
Covers a year with term programs.
The programs could be 3 x 10 weeks for example.
Other combinations are also possible.

Work out what you want to do and get started.
However you might need some type of accreditation.
That's if you want the students to be able to get government grants.
They also might need that if they are going to seek employment.
I assume you are **NOT** going to worry about that.
I don't!

You could provide your own certificate.
This probably will not mean much to government agencies.
It may be important to your students.
What should be more important is that they actually learn something.

Look up some schools on the internet.
They don't have to be art schools to find out what some offer students.
You can start a school from whatever you have done previously.

John Hill (West Sussex UK) suggests finding out as much as you can.
Do this **BEFORE** actually making any hard decisions.
Established your potential clients (children, students, workers, retired).
Are there enough in your catchment area for the desired number of classes.
In the UK, as elsewhere, most people at privately run art classes are retired.

It is also a good idea to do research into the competition notes John.
Are there any other classes currently available in your area?
If so, is there room for more?
What do these classes offer?
More importantly what do you offer that they don't!

Further research is required concerning suitable venues for classes.
Are the venue hire fees reasonable?
Can you book at a time to suit yourself and your potential students?
Is there adequate parking?
Are tables and chairs supplied?
Is the lighting adequate?
Are toilet facilities available? etc.

2. Another set of initials!

TQM stands for Total Quality Management.
In business to-day, and the last decade or so, a major influences is TQM.
Many major corporations have adopted TQM principles.
TQM is a fundamental part of how they do business.

World's best practice is the aim.
The objective is to achieve total quality in everything done.
It's particularly relevant to export industries, with tough overseas competition.
It can be easier to implement in a manufacturing business that some others.
A picture framer could adopt TQM principles more easily than gallery owner.

Making TQM work is not so easy.
The aim is nothing less than perfection.
Think of McDonalds and you'll have the idea.

There are NO mistakes for everything is set out according to standards.
Every Big Mac comes out exactly the same as every other one.
They each take the same time to make too.
There's really no chance of anything going wrong.

Now I know you're probably thinking
'This hasn't anything to do with me, I'm an artist and a teacher!
However, if we look at how TQM works, there may be some lessons for us.

First of all quality is about service standards.
That means you have to know what they are.
And where you are in relation to them.
A decision is made on what determines quality and how it is to be measured.

This could take a little ingenuity, but measure what is meaningful.
There's no point measuring performance of a framer against your sales.
The framer can't do anything about your sales, but the kind of frame might.

You can measure the average time it takes for the framer to fill an order.
You can measure the accuracy of their work.
You might even measure cost savings using different frames or framers.
Some of these will impact on the quality of your service as artist to clients.

But this means measure, not guess.
You can measure the effect of different types of frames on your sales.
Provided the works contained are similar and the outlets are similar.

Actually measure what is important to you.
Quality of the components can be improved against a base measurement.
Count the number of works sold, how big are they, and what are their prices?
These are relevant measurements.
Delete those frames that do not perform, but maintain those that do.
Client satisfaction, as measured by sales, must improve.

In an up-market resort, someone monitors toilets and bathrooms.
There's a checklist to make sure all is in place and in good supply.
That includes tissues, towels, soap, mirrors clean, flowers, and so forth.

You could make a checklist of things to do when enrolling students.
Another for making sure your teachers' classes are run correctly.

If this seems a bit over the top, then think about it like this?
They are tasks that are done regularly, but not daily.
If you write down a routine, it's easier next time, you don't have to reinvent it.
Also you might make improvements and thus streamline your checklist.
Eventually you'll know it quite well and not need to refer to it at all.

But should something happen and someone else has to do the task.
They can use your checklist and perform up to your standard.

The alternative is your school is in trouble and so are your finances.
Your classes are poorly taught.
Students do not re-enroll.

The idea of TQM is to make 'quality' not a word which sounds good.
But performance of actual tasks, even mundane ones, which are identified.
To understand quality in relation to your art school answer these questions.

Who is your customer?
This could be a student, teacher, publisher or some other person.

What does that customer value?
Each customer will have a different set of values.
Work out what they are.
If you are unsure just ask those customers.

What is a 'great course' in their eyes?
Having 'great courses' sets your school apart.
But you can't do it until you know what it is!
Have a clear picture, almost certain to be different for different customers.
Again you could ask some of your clients.

How do you measure that standard of a 'great course'?
This is immediate, observable, ongoing and relevant to an activity.
It must deliver the client's expectations.
It must be easy to measure and understand.
As already mentioned, actual enrollments can be measured.

How do you improve on that result to add more value?
There should be a process of continuing improvement.
Measure whatever you think is an improvement.
Keep records and you'll know whether you are improving or not.

There are steps towards providing great service.
At a basic level, you supply the very minimum, or else there'll be no students.
It's a desired course at the right price for example.
It's an expectation any client takes for granted and is satisfied with.

Perhaps the course has content they're familiar with?
However, go beyond that and provide what is desired.
Then a sense of appreciation can be engendered in the customer.
They are more likely to be satisfied and become loyal.
For example your courses all come with a money back guarantee!

Students aren't satisfied and loyal, but actively promote your school.
That's when they are surprised and delighted by your service.
They're now your patrons.
Perhaps you can give them a special price or an unexpected add-on?

Of course none of this happens by accident.
You must have a vision for your school.
You should be able to spell out that vision.
Often we have a vague idea about where we are heading.
But few art teachers sit down and think it through by writing everything down.
When you are clear about it, you'll know what to do, and what not to do.

Share your vision with anyone who is necessary for its achievement.
If they know you are heading in a certain direction.
They can help you get there so make them part of your team.
They contribute towards the performance standards that delight students.

Often we are pre-occupied with fighting fires.
The immediate takes precedence over the planning and goal-setting.
Things like measurement and self-assessment fall by the wayside.
You should regularly take time out to assess progress.

Quality is about doing ordinary things extraordinarily well.
Quality is not about 'near enough is good enough'.
It's absolutely critical for us if we are to compete in a tough market.
It's something we must constantly think about, or it just won't happen!
But when it happens constantly it becomes a habit which can be built upon.

Focus on TQM principles is essential if the business is to be a success;
John Hill (UK) says this has it has enabled him to 'corner the local market.

3. Do you have a procedures manual?

Most artists certainly will not have one of these.
Most schools do not either but this follows from the quality focus.
Probably most businesses don't, but larger businesses are more likely to.
All franchises have a procedures manual, but they have different names.

That's also why franchises are a very effective business model.
A procedures manual means everyone knows what they are supposed to do.
They can contribute to making the business work.

How should you go about creating one?
The first step is to develop a computer file outlining your business approach.
This includes action steps or procedures taken to do anything important.
Important things are those that just must be done right or a poor job results.
It could be things done a certain way because that's how you do them.

They are a part of your brand or business personality.
They could also be things that are only done occasionally.
Writing what has to be done means you do not forget how to do them.

That's a lot of work, so break it down into manageable chunks.
Initially just create an outline of the main elements of your art school.
You might consider such aspects as classes, marketing, finance, and so on.
Develop a list of procedures to accompany the headings you've decided on.
At this stage you just list those procedures.

Now if you encounter a problem, write it down.
Document the procedures (or steps) to be taken to solve that problem.
Put that onto your loose-leaf procedures manual.

If a problem reappears at a later date, refer to a procedure and follow it.
If changes are needed make them and add the new procedure.
So over time each important procedure gets developed into even better.

If you employ anyone they contribute in a similar way to your manual.
Try to deal with three or four procedures a month (even if no problem).

Eventually everything you do will be in your Procedures Manual.
What you have developed are systems for running your art school.
Anybody can use it so it might even be the basis for franchising!
It will also save considerable wastage of your time.
If people want to know how something is done, just refer them to a manual.

If you document just one procedure a week, that is 50 or so in a year!
If they are the most urgent a large chunk of frustrating situations are gone.
So make a list of the most urgent jobs you do.
Start a Procedures Manual (Rainbow Book) to cover the situations.

4. How do you delegate?

When you have a Procedures Manual delegation is easy.
Arrange procedures according to the various jobs people have.
Delegate by reference to the appropriate section.
This may not seem important right now.
If you employ others to teach it will decide success or failure of any venture.

Delegation is a key to leveraging yourself.
If/when you employ teachers you'll need to delegate.
Basically you get other people to do things for you.

Used effectively you can increase your income *and* free time as well!
In the business-world there is an awareness of the importance of delegation.
This is lacking in our industry as we don't think of ourselves as employers.
The following summarizes the fundamental principles of effective delegation:

If you do what you do best; then delegate or discontinue anything else.
Delegate any tasks that can be performed by a person earning less than you.
If your goal is $100,000 a year, delegate tasks you won't do for $50 an hour.
That frees you to focus time and energy on tasks worth $50 an hour or more.
Time on tasks of less value is inefficient investment of your time and energy.

You might think the mathematics is wrong (like John Hill did also).
To earn $100,000 a year you won't want to work 40 or more hours a week!
Similarly you won't want to work every week of the year or anything like that.
Then you have time to vacation, paint or earn another $100,000!

Now you are thinking like an entrepreneur rather than a teacher.
People who know more than you are more efficient and able to carry out that task in less time.
In my case it's worth paying an accountant.

Define the task clearly.
What is your intended outcome?

You have to be clear about what you want the person to do.
You'd like a teacher, but what exactly do you expect them to do?
Then should you start looking for someone who can and is willing to do that.

Explain the task clearly.
When you find a person for a task, ask them to repeat task details *in writing*.
If their description is not an accurate description of what you want.
Explain differences in detail and again submit their understanding *in writing*.
This step of writing helps enormously in achieving buy-in.
It also helps to make sure you get the outcome you want.
Otherwise they'll do what they think you want, which may not be the same.

Discuss and get agreement on the resources to achieve the task.
There's a problem if you hire a teacher and they submit expense invoices.
Particularly if this hasn't been discussed.

What happens next?
Discuss and agree on consequences of completing or not completing a task.
Are there to be penalties for non-performance, or bonus for superior results?

How much time is there?
You need to define and get agreement on deadline for completion of a task.
There should also be benchmarks by which you can measure progress.
There might be a series of benchmarks for stages to a longer-term objective.

A written understanding is signed by the parties to the arrangement.
Add decisions on resources, consequences, time to the task description.
Psychologically an agreement transforms understanding to commitment

Monitor progress by checking on agreed benchmarks and timeframes.
Do not think your job has been done when they agree to the arrangement.
People have been known not to deliver!

However your delegation turns out, keep your word on consequences.
Do what you said!

Convert the steps to a written guarantee for enrolling students.

Make a list of people and circumstances when delegation is appropriate.

Develop a Ten Point Plan to cover these circumstances.

5. A sample Job Description for an art teacher.

What does a teacher do?
Set out what a teacher has to do in the form of a job description.
Then they should deliver what you expect of them.
OK just what might a Job Description be like?

Position: Teacher

Reports to:
You as head of the art school.

Responsible for:
Outline of teaching duties.
This could be from the Procedures Manual

Duties:
Common tasks for all employees.
List various things that must be done.

Tasks Specific to the Position
This could be from the Procedures Manual
List various things that must be done.

Top priority KPI's
Key Performance Indicators (KPI) refer to important areas.
They are measurable.
They determine why you'd keep this person in this position.
How will they be measured?
Use checklists and/or reporting mechanisms.

Team contribution and accountability
Key actions/updates/tasks completed to assist other team members or peers.
The team depends on these tasks to be completed.
Otherwise they cannot do their job.

Personal attributes
Is responsible.
Conscientious.
Can work unsupervised.
There is a commitment to learn new tasks.
Has a good work ethic.
Is reliable.
Shows initiative.
Helpful.
Open to suggestions.
Honesty.
Skills
Minimum required for teaching position.
At required level.
Minimum education level
Appropriate level of artistic skills
Good communication
Negotiation
Customer Service
?? Yrs. experience in (field)
?? Product knowledge
?? Computing
?? Software

Future development
For next 6 months
Internal training.
Attend conferences.
Reading

Short to medium term objectives
Projects to accomplish rather than ongoing regular tasks.

Regular performance management review and appraisal
Define when, by whom, how often, tools, etc.

Position

Actively participate in weekly/monthly reviews/meetings/
Use key documents and/or manager reports of completed tasks by
individual/team.
Receive semi-annual performance appraisal use Job Description by manager

Staff

Conduct weekly/monthly reviews/meetings using (key documents/reports)
and/or reports of KPIs & goals achievement, individual or team, by myself.
Conduct semi-annual performance appraisal using Job Descriptions &
appraisal agenda by myself & manager.

_____   _____

Teacher Signature   Date

_____   _____

Your Signature   Date

**This job description is the basis/agenda for future Performance
Appraisal meetings.**

Chapter Three: Your focus makes it work.

1. How important is commitment?
2. A laser has power!
3. A painting is not a focus.
4. Like a laser focus is about less NOT more.
5. What is leverage?
6. Leverage yourself!
7. Sell more and make more!
8. Conventional business wisdom is get BIG.
9. What about licensing your courses?

1. How important is commitment?

Alex Carty (South Africa) was at a course sponsored by "Peace Parks".
One of the things Alex heard was this:
Until committed, there's hesitancy, chance to draw back, and ineffectiveness.
Concerning all acts of initiative and creation; there is one elementary truth.
The ignorance of which kills countless ideas and splendid plans.

The moment one definitely commits oneself then fortune moves too.
All sorts of things occur to help that would otherwise never have occurred.
A whole stream of events issues from the decision.
Each unforeseen incident and meeting and material assistance is favourable.
None of which you could have dreamed would have come your way.

Have you experienced how doors open once a commitment is made?
Have you forsaken a steady predictable occupation?
Did you fear the risky business of earning a living as an art teacher?

I tend to think of this as an illustration of the power of having a focus.
If you can add value to everything you do, success will come your way.
Clay can become an article of beauty, because of the potter's skill.

Your school can have added value too.
I am really talking about your ideas, thoughts, plans and actions.
Let them grow and multiply and let your dreams guide you as well.
Set goals for each day, then a week, and a month, and even a year, or more.
If setting objectives consider your best effort in the past and improve on it.

Your objectives cannot be too high or ambitious.
Occasionally you may not quite achieve these lofty ambitions.
But you can learn from this and move forward again.

You have total control of your goals.
But without dreams your goals can never become a reality.
With them, anything is possible.
Particularly if you move forward so each day improves on yesterday.

Let others know what your dreams are for they may be able to help.
There'll be motivation to persist; knowing others are aware of your dreams.

As your goals are attained, set new ones and make them public too.
Constantly strive to improve what you do.
This is the way to add value to everything including your art school.

But having a focus does not guarantee success.
Well not straight away at least.
In the short term, narrowing focus may even cost business opportunities.
For you'll turn away chances because they do not fit in your plans.

For example someone wants to learn to paint in watercolour.
But you are only teaching painting in oils now.
Because oils are your focus you will turn down the watercolour opportunity.
So you might lose students by dropping certain kinds of courses.

A powerful focus is almost never effective in the short term.
If this were not true then every business would be enormously successful.

All you would need to do is try a number of different approaches.
What works, keep doing it, or replace what doesn't work with something else.
Sooner or later you've established a successful business or career.

Many businesses, even artists, actually employ this strategy.
But it doesn't work!
What tends to work in the short term doesn't tend to work in the long term.
Any business run by chasing immediate success, ultimately heads for failure.
You can only head away from where you start!

You need to have the courage to make a focusing decision.
Then wait for the market to react to your move.
It won't happen overnight, but it will happen so you have to be patient.

Persistence is the key to success.
Make the correct decision and then keep moving forward with it.
At first progress will be slight, but momentum will gather.

This probably sounds difficult to do.
But a focus is to activity, as a laser is to light.
Concentrated light is very powerful and does things diffused light can't.
It's the same for another power source, your energy
Focus your energy and you'll achieve what others consider impossible.

In the past, Joe Bloggs had classes for married females.
In other words that's where he looked for his student base.
In the next year Joe directs more promotional effort at 2 growing segments,
They are retirees and high net worth Individuals (female).

Joe, being a local can gains considerable share of these two segments.
That's because of his local knowledge.
He intends to structure his advertising specifically for each segment.
He utilizes a broad range of promotional options to communicate.

Joe plans to promote along these lines:
To established families he emphasizes top quality and value for money.
To the retiree segment Joe will emphasize his expertise.
He'll offer a special painting pack for anyone who enrolls.
To high net worth segment Joe introduces and emphasize premium courses.
He'll also place a special emphasis on female clients in this segment

Finding a focus is easy.
It's easier for an art school than a large business.
There's a danger with the big organization that any focus is lost in the crowd.
Committees can't find simple ideas, only complex ones.
A focus is always simple.
Just think about the ideas and then decide.

Typical for an art school is to produce good painters.
But the more specific your focus the more you'll become like the laser.
Decide what you'll teach, what are your fees, how long is the course?
For example how about a focus on teaching portraiture in oils in five weeks?
Then achieve this laser-like artistic goal in a series of small steps.
Large steps are daunting and you'll probably not get there.

These days the acronym USP is common.
A Unique Selling Position, is what your art school that no-one else has.
List all the things you do and find those, or a combination, that set you apart.
This may be the same as your focus, or it may only be your marketing focus.
Whatever, your focus is about what you do, whether marketed or not.

2. A laser has power!

If you want to do well, you should be where other people like you are.
It's a collective focus and it's powerful.
Broken Hill is probably as unlikely a place for an artist as any other.
Yet many artists live there and I presume make a living.

The sheer volume of artists attracts more artists.
This in turn attracts others interested in art and what the artists are doing.
They are largely rendering the outback.

It's a phenomenon that will continue to grow.
The focus is continually reinforcing itself.
Santa Fe is similar in USA and there are art focused areas through the world.
Same with cars, jewellery, fashion, telemarketing, gambling, red light areas.
It doesn't just happen in big cities for small towns have an 'auto alley'!

Rather than discourage others, and retiring into your ivory tower,
Encourage them into towers near yours in the heart of your area's art focus.
Except your group of towers are all art schools!
There's strength in numbers because of the clarity of focus provided.
When you have a focus, like the laser, you create a powerful perception.
Perception of value is linked to your focus and lies in the mind of a student.
Thus a focus is self-reinforcing.

An unfocused business will try to achieve balance.
All things are treated as being of equal importance.
Attention is shuffled to make sure there is a rationing of effort.
An artist pays as much attention to painting, framing, selling and researching.
Add to that the search for mastery in a range of media!

But when you have a focus you know what to do.
For example you know what kind of teachers you want or need to retain.
You'll know what research you need to do, or new courses to introduce.

People gravitate to businesses, artists or art schools with a focus.
Think of cities and suburbs where there are artists and galleries.
These areas attract an infrastructure that helps to maintain their specialty.
Galleries are alive and prospering as the focus attracts the right clientele.
In other areas, a gallery might find it hard to survive no matter how well run!

In a world where knowledge is rapidly expanding, a focus is essential.
With no focus you won't stay on top of all developments in the art business.
That's because no one can stay on top of all things.
A focus can direct you to those areas most likely to be of benefit to you.
Without a focus it is impossible to dominate.
Focus lets you to sit on ever-expanding knowledge you are the expert.
Anyone interested in oil painting wants to attend your school has that focus!
You'll automatically put most effort, and dollars, where there might be results.

Focus means you put resources into future products or services.
You may have to still deal with activity from the past
But your focus will make it obvious that they are not part of any future plans.

Focus really means moving from yesterday's ideas to the future.
In the short term you may need to deal with old projects in an efficient way.
This could even mean canning them as soon as possible.
It would definitely mean no new enrollments in such courses.
That shouldn't distract you from putting most attention on to-morrow's focus.

Better to be inefficient but powerfully focused market-oriented school.
Than cover all bases as you can't change direction if there is no direction.

Do you really have a focus to your art school?
You can write it down and use it as a guide to effective decision making.
That means your focus is your future!
The main task of your art school is work to your future goals, so they happen.
Day to day things should be secondary to those.
If you don't do this, then your hopes and aspirations are being left to chance.

Prediction your future and take specific steps to make that happen!
Many years ago, Volvo selected 'safety' as a focus.
They made a prediction about their future and the direction of their industry.
They also decided how their present (then) activities would be carried out.

Deciding about where you want to head is not just wishful thinking.
Look at what you are doing to-day.
What single service, product, or idea is your best hope for the future?
That becomes the basis for your future.

It's that simple!
It's also hard.
The hard part is making the right selection from the different things you do.
It's hard for you won't know you've been right until a lot of time has gone.
By then it's probably too late to return to one of the other options.
Never-the-less this is what you must do.

As time goes by there's an upward spiral supporting the decision.
Your focus allows you to develop in ways not previously possible or seen.

One scenario might concern which media your school should focus on.
At an early stage you'll want to teach about a variety.
They're all exciting for students to explore and discover.
This is a learning phase for your school and is important.

At some point you make a professional decision about the media focus.
It doesn't matter, just as long as you enjoy teaching about say oil painting.
By spending more time with this particular material you'll get to know more.
You do more than those who divide time on different media.
The same kinds of comments apply to subject or style specialization too.
Some people want your watercolour courses and won't enroll in oil classes.

Such a decision can have short term penalties!
But these penalties are temporary.
The longer you run a particular focus, the less important such penalties are.

You'll be increasingly sought out for what you do, do.
In art teaching it's best to be good at something than average at many things.
If you don't focus on something you may not have much of a future!

But sooner or later even the most powerful focus can become obsolete.
That's when it's necessary to re-focus.
This doesn't mean focus is fashionable that can change every second year.
It just means inevitably a focus will eventually be out of date.

It may take years or even decades.
In some industries it will be more rapid.
Probably our industry doesn't change much, not as much as some think.

A focus loses power if the environment in which it operates changes.
A way to illustrate this idea is to think about the life of some famous artists.
Pierre Renoir is was someone whose focus was constant for many years.
He re-evaluated his artistic focus toward the end of his life.
Age and failing eyesight meant a different kind of painting emerged.
Many other artists' careers demonstrate this process (Picasso) too.
Those who lived short lives didn't adjust focus at all (Raphael, van Gogh).

It's also easy to think of artists who changed focus needlessly.
Their career became unstuck and they are not famous but we all know them.
Often this is a result of an artist being bored with what they currently do.
They look for something different, rather than adopting a new focus.

What about you?
Are you still living with yesterday's strategies?
The future belongs to those who develop a powerful focus to-day.

3. A painting is NOT a focus.

It's the rationale behind the painting that is (or is not) a focus.
Volvo makes cars, but that's not the company's focus for the focus is safety.
BMW, also a car manufacturer, is focused on producing driving machines.
The difference in focus is why their cars are different.
It's also why they appeal to different segments of the car buying public.

A product can't be a focus unless it's unique and is a monopoly.
To say your focus is teaching watercolour is not sufficient.
That's because there is competition from others who teach watercolours.

What your teaching is in someone's mind the others are opposite.
If your classes are expensive then the opposition is cheap.
If your classes are low priced then others are up-market.
If your watercolour focus is on softness then others are precise and sharp.
Large works are contrasted to miniatures and so on.
Each time they occupy someone's mind as alternatives.

This phenomenon is known a segmentation of the market.
A market (paintings/classes) is broken into a number of different segments.
There is **NO** market segment bought by all people.
The dominant seller may try to be 'all things to everybody'.
But that's different and is likely to result in a loss of focus.
The risk is they become nothing special to anybody.

Artists working all mediums, style variety and subjects, runs this risk.
They compete against artists who only paint abstract oils or watercolours.
This artist can only sell well if there is no opposition, like in their own gallery.
Such an artist should decide which aspect of the market they will focus on.
Support that decision by, suitable pricing, framing, promotion and distribution.
That's what focus is about.
If you're not willing to walk away from a business segment there is no focus.
Imagine a '$10,000 and drive away with no more to pay' Rolls Royce?
Running an art school is exactly the same.

Focus is not the same as a strategy.
Many businesses have a strategy.
They want to become major players in their field for example.
But strategies, or mission statements, do not limit what the company does.

A focus is about narrowing the perspective of a business.
An intention not to cover all eventualities, but dominate a market segment.
There is strength when you can dominate a segment of the market.
There's no power when you are just a small player in a big market.
Then you have no control over your destiny, it is shaped by bigger players.
You are somewhat like a small leaf floating in a stream.
It could be a pleasant journey, but you've little control over where you finish.

Let's review the focus concept once more.
Some artists wish to master all media and it is a tantalizing challenge.
Mastery is time spent on a task multiplied by the degree of intelligent effort?
A multiple-media artist spends time working with each of the different media.
They achieve a particular level of mastery at each of them.

Say we clone this artist, so we have one for each of the different media.
Each of the clones works intelligently for the same total amount of time.
But only in a single medium, rather than the whole range.
The clones have exactly the same levels of intelligence.
Will they achieve similar, lesser or greater mastery than the artist has?

It's much more difficult to master a range of disciplines and succeed.
Energy is applied in less successful areas so they're brought up to the mark.
This reduces time spent on those areas the artist does best.
The lack of focus reduces the artistic energy applied to any other disciplines.
It is dissipated instead and I've only been talking of the artistic difficulties.

There's also the marketing problem.
A person, who tries to cover all artistic bases, doesn't stand for anything.
The more specific the focus of an artist the easier it is to market that artist.

An art school is in exactly the same position.
Perhaps you teach in all mediums to a reasonable level?
What can you say that makes your teaching stand out from others like you?

How can your classes stand out from others where each is a specialist?
But they will continue to improve at a greater rate than you can match!
You will inevitably be left behind.

Let's say you teach oil painting of local buildings of historical interest.
The more specific you get, the easier you are to promote.
This is basically the case for specialization.
Focus makes it possible.

It's good to have a strategy of the general direction of your art school.
It's better to be clear about the focus of the business than lofty aims for it.
Artists who do something better than anyone receive acclaim and rewards.
The same applies to teachers!

Sometimes a school thinks they have a focus with a uniform theme.
They hang everything they do under the theme but it's usually a set of words.
It is possible to develop a set of words to fit any scenario.
A school might say 'We are a local art school,' thinking they have a focus.
This really might mean your school is in a particular place.
But you teach in all sorts of mediums, covering a range of styles, etc.
Then the only local component is where your school is.

There's no focus in that!
It would be different if the school only taught painting of local subjects.
Or made the materials your students use locally.
Or only allowed local students.
Or some other way the localness is emphasized in what is done.

4. Like a laser focus is about less NOT more.

By its nature a focus doesn't cover everything you might be able to do.
It's a point of attack towards the future of your artistic business (school).

At any time an art school has three types of courses,
Yesterday's courses.

Today's courses, which should have most of your students.
Today's courses should also be producing the bulk of your profits.
To-morrow's courses are being developed and are your future.

Your focus, what you sell, and how you make money might be different.
A focus is the bridge that takes you from to-day to to-morrow.
You teach painting in oils and in the future you see acrylic as the way to go.
Focus lets you bridge the gap and make the change possible even profitable.

A focus can and should change as circumstances change.
Nothing stays the same long enough for you to stay singularly focused.
The objective of your focus should be to lead you in a coherent direction.

Having established school goals, focus until you achieve them.
Do not let your focus slip - focus sorts the professional from the hobbyist.
Maintaining focus will mean you are prepared to make sacrifices.
But that's only if a particular activity does not lead you towards your goal.
To continue this now will only divert you from achieving your goal.

You may break down your goal into smaller sub-goals.
Progressively work at those as you advance towards the major objective.
The oil-painter student could just paint in black and white, for a year or two.
Add another colour to the range, and later another colour is introduced.

Think how such a process is likely to lead to mastery of the materials.
Particularly if similar subjects and a limited range of brushes are in the plan.
This illustrates focus and also the scientific method!

Focus is the characteristic of winners in any field.

Don't be sidetracked, but stay on your chosen pathway.

This doesn't mean you can't change your focus from time to time.

You can, but only if your goals are first changed.

These only change for something better (you achieve your initial plans).

Or because you set your sights too high to start with so now they're realistic.

But still in the same direction.

5. What is leverage?

Leverage is a marketing idea based on a similar principle in physics.
Levers allow us to magnify the results of effort.
Any activity magnifying the results of a marketing effort is leverage.

An example is to borrow 100% of the money to make an investment.
The return on the investment is greater than interest on the money borrowed.
Then you have used the principle of leverage.

With marketing the same effort can have variations of approach.
They create results 10%, 50%, or 250% better than a standard strategy.
These different results represent the leverage from the various strategies.

For example, how you frame your work is a marketing strategy.
You could frame your works in gold with tasteful cream slips or mats.
This is a more expensive approach (than your standard framing).

If you sell more works, or higher prices, then you leveraged your return.
There may have been a cost increase of say, $15 per frame.
This is offset by an extra $350 per painting you can now charge (whatever).
As well as the increased prospect of a sale.

It costs a certain amount to run an advert.
In the local paper, or a magazine, or send out a sales letter, or invitation.
It costs this amount whether you obtain one, three, or twenty students.
But each approach could be produced in a variety of different ways.

Not all would produce identical results.
Variations could be 2, 5, 10, even 200 times greater for your marketing $.
Than the least effective method, but the cost is the same in each case!

It costs the same to get a student to a course whether they enrol once.
Or come back repeatedly.
The real question isn't so much whether leverage works, it's how you do it?

Like many things the answer is quite simple, but does take time.
You must deliberately test variations in the actual marketplace.
Test all the ideas you have and let your students tell you all about leverage.
They let you know by how they do or do not respond.
You are in a good position to conduct tests as you have complete control.
All factors concerning the marketing of your courses are decided by you.
Unless you delegate them to someone else.

Don't tell the market what they can do but test variations.
Then see what the best response is.
Basically you need to take a leaf out of the scientist's book.
They conduct research into all sorts of things.
Scientific research limits the variables being investigated and controls others.

Have one course on sale in a standard format.
Each time the course is introduced vary the fee.
Over a period of time it is from less than you expect to considerably more.
Eventually you'll discover the highest price you can sell courses like this at.

Now try the same process with another course.
But start at your highest fee and see if you can go any higher.
When you understand pricing of this course, go back to another course.
Repeat the process.
Try other variations, whilst keeping the price at your now established level.
This process continues as long as you are a professional teacher.
Testing never stops!

But a result of testing is you will understand the principles of leverage.
Well as they apply to your courses and marketing.
For example use a standard promotional format.
Each time use a different approach with a small number of students.
With and without a coloured image for example.
Compare the results and on the basis of this test again.

Eventually you'll know (not guess) what gives a best result.

That's now your standard approach.

It should give considerably better result than previous standard (or why do it).

But even then, still conduct research looking for even better results.

You can acquire from testing a most powerful pieces of knowledge.

Find out why students and potential students actually enroll in your courses.

What benefit do they get from being taught by you?

Is their idea of value, the same as yours?

Which one counts?

Write down one aspect of your marketing.

Now consider how you could leverage what you are presently doing.

What research may need to be done in conjunction?

6. Leverage yourself!

Can people read your mind?
You have to let them know what you can do for them.
For many people that's not easy.

Let's say you do know how you can help your prospects.
Get someone to interview you.
Make a tape, CD, DVD, or some other recording?

You provide the questions though.
Get the interviewer to ask why people should enroll with you?
Now you can tell about your USP (Unique Selling Proposition)?
Mention your specific areas of expertise?
Now a prospect might find out how you can help them.

From the recording it is easy to create PDF documents.
There might also be a checklist for the prospect.
There could also be an article for them to read.
You can leverage yourself!
Send the document to anyone who would be interested in your teaching.
Use a checklist if talking to a prospect but don't worry about perfection, do it.

Remind people what you have done for them.
Also tell them why to let them know they're appreciated.
They can't read your mind can they?
So how can **YOU** help your prospects?
What effect would that have?

In business, the best way to attract customers is provide better value.
This is better value than the opposition, or better than normally expected.
Obvious ways are a cheaper price or better quality for the same price.
Another way is to provide an extra service or product at little or no extra cost.
When this is done a business gives better value by providing an 'add-on'.
For example, buy one widget and get another free.

They're basically bonuses people receive with a purchase.
Similar propositions include buy a Big Mac and get French Fries for 1/2 price.
They're everywhere because quite simply they work.

John Hill (West Sussex, UK) suggests the very best of bonuses.
In the UK the majority of privately run art classes are for retired people.
It's the same elsewhere too.
So now there is time available to do things they haven't been able to before.
They also want to escape the boredom of being stuck at home.
Many 'students' attend art classes for a sense of belonging too.
That means the social side of the teaching business is important.

The social aspect of running art classes can be enhanced considerably.
Have a stimulating (socially/artistically), relaxed and friendly environment.
This can be as simple as providing coffee and biscuits after each class.
Also arrange trips and excursions to places of artistic interest.

Attention to the social aspects of your classes is financially rewarding.
You can charge more for your courses.
You can also promote those as benefits for prospective students.
Any artist can struggle to make a living running their own art school.
If they do not have the necessary organizational and social skills
It's best to be a competent all-round artist, organizer and entertainer.
You can get away as a mediocre artist if you give people a good time.

Are add-ons like discounts?
'Add-ons' are a different kettle of fish from discounts.
To take advantage a student makes a commitment to enroll, at full price.
You still make the full amount on the sale itself.
Provided you get your money back for the 'add-on', or it actually costs little.
With a discount you reduce your profit in the hope of extra sales.

An 'add-on' is still profitable whatever the volume of sales.
'Add-on' can stimulate extra sales over and above what normally is expected.

Do any dangers depend on how it is done?

It's possible to use an 'add-on' as a standard sales method.

But there's a danger it will lose effectiveness over time.

Eventually the two elements are seen by potential students as a normal unit.

This may still be good value compared with other businesses.

But it won't be in terms of your own offerings.

You may attract new students but are decreasingly effective for regulars.

This isn't necessarily bad, but it could be better.

Particularly because regular students are probably the best clients.

It's much more likely you'll use 'add-ons' for special situations.

In the real world this is what happens too.

You can't get 1/2 price French Fries all the time, only special occasions.

The 'add-on' used by McDonalds for extra customers when they want them.

It's not likely to be during school holidays, is it?

Like McDonalds 'add-ons' can help with sales or marketing problems.

Getting people to enroll in your course for the first time may be difficult.

This is particularly so, if you're new to the potential student.

Provide an incentive or 'add-on' to help potential students break that barrier?

As in most businesses conditions apply before people get the 'add-on'.

It's not usually sufficient that someone just buys.

They must be certain kinds of people (children),

Or buying at a particular price level ($10 pizza),

Or a certain kind of product (Big Mac), and so forth.

Think on these lines and there are many areas where 'add-ons' help.

You certainly can add to your bottom-line with 'add-ons'!

7. Sell more and make more!

Increase the frequency of purchase.
That means you increase the number of times people buy stuff from you.
But you need a back end product to sell.
That could be to simply sell another course to your existing students.
If they bought once they'll buy repeatedly if you supply a good experience.

You can sell more and more expensive stuff on the back end.
Provide ever more expensive levels of courses, products and services.
Develop those sales from your front end sale and students are likely to buy.

Start with short classes and build to expensive courses or workshops.
Create double, triple, quadruple platinum courses for increasing fees.
They can become more exclusive too.
Some people will enroll just because they want the more expensive option.

If you place a ladder in front of somebody they want to climb it.
If you know there's another level you could be at you want to get there.
They'll buy them.

BUT you MUST deliver massive value.
A way to create a back end is develop a gold edition of a course you selling.
Then offer that to your existing student base.
Also offer that as an up-sell to all new clients coming in.

You have created an increased frequency of purchase.
A previous a one time student now buys something else from you.
For all future clients you're increasing the size of the transaction.
They pay more for the gold edition of the standard course you sell now.

Another thing you can do on the back end is to sell live events.
For example, if you sell oil painting lessons you can also sell studio visits.
This could be to your studio.
But arrange a studio inspection tour and visit a number of artists' studios.

Naturally in this example all would be oil painters.
Sell that for a little bit of money or for a lot of money, whatever you want.

Another possibility is running live seminars.
This can be extremely lucrative but they can also be extremely risky.
They are always a lot of work.
They work best if you've a large database which makes seminars less risky.
The marketing cost which would be needed is reduced considerably.

It is helpful to have a meeting planner.
Good ones will save you far more than they'll ever cost you.
The reason is they have influence with hotels and other conference venues.
Otherwise the venue will charge you every way they can.
You probably won't know what's happened until it's too late.
A good meeting planner won't let that happen to you.
Get someone who does the major venues.
They takes care of every detail and makes the best deals.

8. The conventional business wisdom is get BIG.

Big = success.
But perhaps for artists it is different?
It all depends on how you define success!
What about teaching art?
Can that get bigger?

There is a real estate developer who does only one development a year.
It's not unusual for others to do ten or one hundred deals a year.
In the case of the first developer, he might look at thousands of opportunities.
But find maybe one hundred that are pretty good but one is great though!

Just one development and makes more money than doing them all.
He can do it better too.
Because his objective isn't volume he can choose only the best.
He does only the best he is continually offered the very best opportunities.
It's an upward spiral!

An art teacher could take just a few students.
They might even be professional artists.
His life and reputation is not cluttered with low-budget, run-of-the-mill artists,
He increases his chances of getting great results, just like the developer.
This is the role of the artist coach.

Now take a look at your student list.
What would happen if you fired half your students?
Get rid of those who pay late, give you a hard time and want your time free.
They are never the source of positive referrals either.
Would your art teaching business improve?
Even these days it surely would.

Sell more and more to an ever larger client base may not be a success!
But if overheads drop then there's less pressure to take the wrong students.
You can wait for the right ones instead.

In any business we can't do everything.
But by leaving alone the lower levels of possible choices our profit goes up,
In addition we dramatically improve the quality of other aspects of our lives.
This kind of thinking has special relevance to art teacher coaches.
It's also important for portrait artists and those who accept commissions.

You might recall the Pareto Principle (80/20 rule).
Or David Ricardo's "Theory of Comparative Advantage of Nations"?
Ricardo suggested specialization leads to wealth.
Self-sufficiency produced poverty.
The developer and architect are using the Law of Comparative Advantage.

Do less and earn more but you could incur a loss of opportunity cost.
Your time and energy should provide the highest possible return,
Aim for the top students, charge top fees, and make courses exclusive!

Compare that with many students for a low fee client base.
Even then your earnings will be meager so it really isn't worth the trouble.
It is easy to see where you should head.
How are you going to do it and do you have the determination?

Another idea is combining projects.
Take the ideas you've been introduced to but in different combinations.
There is little added work - rewrite a sales letter, take little things out and put different things in.

Such an approach can be sent to prospects.
It will earn money.
But the money isn't as important as the leads that are gathered.
Just repackage things in a different order and you have little additional work.
But you have a range of new different products.

9. What about licensing your courses?

You might license and write training courses for royalties.
There are several different ways to license your courses.
Write course materials for a company you sell to duplicates and delivers.

You can always provide a 'train-the-trainer' class.
If you devise a course, you might want to make sure it's delivered properly.
As part of your deal, you could train their trainers for money.
Then you get paid to do that, as well as the course materials and royalties.

I'm not an Intellectual Property attorney / lawyer.
For money for material you might need an Intellectual Property specialist.
They understand licensing legalities.
But make sure yours knows about teaching, courses and art.
Some license music and could be clueless about course materials.
So find somebody good that's already done it.

Another kind of licensing is a little bit different.
Sponsorship of your student materials like books and other training materials.
A company pays to be involved or included in your books.
You need to think who would want to be in front of my students?'
This might be an art supply shop and picture framer is another sponsor.
Carriers who specialize in freighting artworks could be another.
You've got to think, who would want to be in front of your clients?

Have different people paying money every time you run a course.
That's if you have the sponsors and they are non-competitive.
These people are also potential licensees for your book and help distribute it.
The more books you distribute, the higher the license fee goes.

Another way to license is to sell your courses to training companies.
These would usually be ones who want new topics.
Those kinds of places sometimes buy course materials.

Another way is as a curriculum for colleges.
You may not know of people buying a curriculum but they start somewhere.

Instead of doing a course by yourself link with a university or college.
They are all looking for additional revenue streams.
If you can go there and provide a course, they could put it in their catalogue.
That's as long as everybody's happy and you suit the powers that be.
They'll name your course in their catalogue.
That way you develop a curriculum and are still the teacher.

If they use your material then they'll need supplies for their students.
Every semester, they order a more of them.

Chapter Four: Wrapping up.

1. Are you a revolutionary?

Historically, artists have had a reputation as revolutionaries.
If your plans involve changes you might be treading a revolutionary path.
Perhaps you may not be revolutionary in the same way that Picasso was.
But there's still a chance you'll seem revolutionary to someone.

Maybe you have some new ideas that you wish to try?
It doesn't matter where new ideas came from; it's what you do that counts.
Naturally you should think these ideas through, so they might work.
You should know what you have to do and why.

You should understand how all parts of the new initiative operate.
Write everything down and you can see if your thinking has inconsistencies.
Put things in diagrams, to see the sequence of events that should take place.
Let's say you have your new idea all sorted out.
You will introduce some new courses or whatever has taken your fancy.

Should you have an impact statement?
People who want to do new things with land must these days do this.

They must commission an environment impact statement.
It's a study of the effect on the environment, from a proposed use of the land.
You don't have to do this, but you could prepare a people impact statement.

It's the likely effect of changes on people connected with your school.
They could be past, present and future students.
In other words what happens when you implement proposed changes?
For there's one thing you can be sure of, and that's there will be an effect.

What happens if you don't do this?
My past includes new ideas about things in different fields.
Sometimes I encountered hostility.
At the time this surprised me as I wasn't even expecting opposition.
In each case I thought I had a practical, sensible solution to a problem.
Many people were quick to realize this and benefit from it.

But there were other people who did not and didn't seem to want to.
I couldn't understand why.
I could appreciate others with different points of view to argue their case.
In fact I could learn from that but they weren't doing this.

The opposition was quite aggressive!
In looking back (marvelous thing hindsight), I can now see a common trend.
I didn't even realize what I was suggesting or proposing, was revolutionary.
I just thought of them as sensible, practical ideas to solve a problem.
That's why the opposition surprised me.

It's also why the opposition was strong!
The strongest proponents for the current beliefs fight for them.
They will not give in lightly.
Logic, demonstration, or other ways to present new ideas do not work.
They will work with people who do not have a strong commitment though!
But not with the 'true believers' of the present orthodoxy.

As people switch to the new idea, the threatened leaders fight stronger.
They have more to lose than any gain offered.

It has always been like this, and always will be.
Perhaps you aren't quite thinking of going that far?
If you change from something to something different people are threatened.
They'll be those who are the biggest fans of your present activity.

Expect opposition from these people.
Certainly not enrollments, just because they've been students before.
Perhaps they'll tolerate one or two different things, but not a complete switch.
For these students you have become a revolutionary.

Why would you change from a successful approach to something new?
Probably the most common reason is that they feel the need for change.
There simply are other things they'd like to do.
That's OK if you're a student, or amateur artist for you only please yourself.

As someone running an art school you must also consider your clients.
That's why you might need a people impact statement.
You need some idea of the likely effect on your students and teachers.
That's if you introduce changes they might perceive as revolutionary.

How the people impact statement (PIS) can help?
The results of a PIS will influence how the school and courses are marketed.
It will not necessarily be what is taught (that is a different matter entirely).
You may still go ahead with a major switch in direction.
At least you know you may need a new student base for the new courses.

But you may not even go ahead with any of the proposed new courses.
That's because you'd rather keep your present students.
It's not easy to attract new students.
Even more so if you've alienated the current ones with your changes.
Attachment to the present approach outweighs any desire to try new ideas.
Others may follow both paths, but adopt different marketing approaches.

These days I'm much more cautious than I used to be.
I still get new ideas (don't we all) on various things, some of which are here.
To develop a project I now know implementation is as important as the idea.
By implementation, I mean how it's presented to other people.
Particularly people who're likely to be involved with strong but different views.

Caution could be part-introduce a new course within a current course.
Introduce new elements as an experiment and ask people for their reactions.
Then introduce people gradually to a new idea but in a non-threatening way.
Depending on their reaction you could broaden this introduction in the future.

Do you consider change related to three levels of teaching activity?
At any time you should be working on three levels.
There are the courses you've done in the past which are being phased out.
Your current courses provide a substantial proportion of your income.
There's also your future, which is where you want to head.
If different from your present courses, this should be introduced gradually.
Use a great deal of thought and planning.

2. Value what you know!

Many people undervalue what they know.
Because it's familiar they assume their knowledge is more common than it is.
They also assume therefore that it's probably not worth much either.
But package your knowledge properly and there could be rewards for you.
Don't underestimate the value of the knowledge and experience you have.
This is the basis for your teaching.

If someone asks about your painting, do you tell them everything?
You do because you are enthusiastic and just want to share your knowledge.
But stop for a moment and think, about what you have just done.
How many years did you take acquiring this knowledge?
What has it cost over those years, in time, courses, and so on?
Why should, in a business sense, someone benefit from this for free?

It's not free if you actually do some work such as a commission!
But when you provide information it usually is.
This is the basis for your teaching which is being undermined.

Can you get free knowledge from an accountant, doctor, or solicitor?
Generally you make an appointment and pay for hard-earned information.
But an artist you will usually provide your knowledge for free.
Why the difference - are you not also a professional?

People like coming to your studio.
So they can see where you work and get to talk to you about what you do.
Artists do not usually charge for this.
You should, charge or the person gets for nothing something they value.
The best way is add % to the price if a work is bought from the studio (10%).

Most artists do not value what they're giving away.
That's why they do not realize how much the recipient values it either.
Perhaps the recipient doesn't value it, because the artist hasn't either.
Packaged your expertise and experience can generate new prospects.

It could also be a new income stream for you.
Spend time writing a report on (say) '27 ways to frame an artwork.'
Place an ad for this in a suitable publication.
You could give the report away and obtain leads for your course in return.
Sell the report and gain income as well as students.

This could lead to other reports.
This idea could be changed a little, depending on your particular expertise.
The main point is that there are other ways to use your knowledge.
Not just doing a job for someone and getting paid.
This is the basis for your teaching.

There's a chance you become an authority on the subject you write on.
You certainly will if you keep it up.
This has great advantage as you are in an industry that's price competitive.

An authority can charge and obtain more.
People will feel confident buying from you because you are the expert.
Because of your reports, they can better appreciate and value what you do.
This is the basis for your teaching.

How do you write a report?
If you are a watercolour artist write on how to paint, frame or hang them.
Maybe buy paints, or understand what the artist does with watercolour.
There is material from paint suppliers to use in addition to what you know.

Convert all this into your own customer-focused language.
Perhaps a 40-point checklist, print the number needed with a laser printer.
Put the report into a binder to add to the presentation.

Make sure what you write is genuinely helpful.
There is a temptation to write a sales piece, but you want to help, not sell.
Running courses, and teaching, are other ways to package your knowledge!
So what could you be considered an expert on?
Which means decide how your knowledge could be packaged for teaching.

Of course writing may not be exactly your field.

Get someone to write, but tell them what to write and put your name on it.

Another way is to be the TV expert.

This will work better if you live in a rural area.

Local TV will need a local art person to make comments from time to time. You can be the person.

That's how many national TV identities got their start.

3. How does skill develop?

I heard a speech by John Brown from the University of Newcastle.
Brown talked about the culture of change within an organization.
I looked at my notes later and saw he also referred to something else.
He used this diagram to illustrate the process of change.

Flexible	Responsive
Effective	Efficient
Control	Predictable
Uncontrolled	Unpredictable

At its lowest level change is uncontrolled and unpredictable as a result.
Then as some control is asserted predictability is a consequence.
The first item in ascending line order, is the degree of control over change.
The second factor is the results that follow, again in ascending order.

The two requirements to move up the ladder are time and practice.
John Brown's interest was about change within an organization.
His model gives an answer to something we're more likely to be interested in.
How does skill, perhaps in watercolour painting, develop?
Let's have a look?

Performance of any task is related to practice at that task.
Initially it is uncontrolled and the results unpredictable.
People beginning watercolour will know what that means.
With more practice comes control and we can predict what might happen.
Our past experience lets us do this.

Where are you on this scale?

But developing skill takes time.

For some it takes a lot of time.

It's obvious when observe children learn to play a sport, or read, or paint.

Adults learning the same things tend to be impatient.

They usually do not allow sufficient time for skill to develop.

The sport of body building illustrates what should take place.

The athlete completes many lifts of weights over a lengthy period of time.

Small increments of additional weight are applied at regular intervals.

Eventually the weight-lifter builds sufficient strength to lift very heavy weights.

Weights that would be impossible at the beginning of this training process.

All those factors Brown talked about are forms of behaviour.

Skills are basically practiced behaviours.

That's what the experienced weight-lifter has attained.

Brown's model is useful to understand how our artistic skills develop.

We gain an insight about what we might still need to work towards.

If you are half way up the ladder you an think there are no more steps to go.

You might stay at that level if you choose, but it is a choice.

But what if you wish to develop a higher level of skill?

What works is many repetitions with small increases in difficulty.

For artistic skills 200 small experimental exercises beats a major work.

Do you intend to develop skills in your students?

Many repetitions with small increments of difficulty are then necessary.

But maintaining enthusiasm over a lengthy period of time is also necessary.

What will you do about that?

4. What is quality?

We all think they can tell a high quality product from a low quality one.
But in reality things are not always so obvious.
Does a Rolex watch keep better time than a Seiko?
Are you sure?
Does a Mercedes have fewer mechanical problems than a Kia?
Are you certain about that?
Does a Montblanc pen write better than a Bic?
Does Coke taste better than Pepsi?
Is your teaching better than mine?
How do you know?

Quality is an idea that is widespread and sincerely believed in.
The way to a better school is to develop better quality courses.
But is this always so?
Building courses on the idea of quality is like building a house on sand.
Sand shifts!
You can build whatever idea of quality you might have into your courses.
But that will have little to do with enrollment success.

Is there any correlation between quality and sales then?
If Coke outsells Pepsi then it must be a better quality cola?
Is that true and how do you know?

Consumer magazines like "Choice" rank similar products on quality.
They use a range of quite objective measures.
But these have little correlation with sales success.
These tests might actually show that quality does not translate into sales.
Why is this?

Go shopping for anything and look for a quality product or service.
The price is right, it's good value and you're likely to buy you have money.
People enrolling in courses are no different.
It seems to make sense to have some focus on a quality course doesn't it?

But where does the idea of quality actually exist?
It's an idea in the student's mind it's not something in the course at all!
So it's actually a perception.
A quality product or service is building this perception in a prospect's mind.
Tiffany did it with their packaging.

Narrow your focus and it is easier to build the quality idea.
You are a specialist (portrait artist, whatever) rather than a generalist.

Specialists are seen to know more and be worth more than a generalist.
If you doubt this just think about doctors in this context.
Does a heart surgeon know more than a general practitioner?
Many people think so.
To be successful a narrow focus is a better track to develop a quality image.

A key factor in building a high quality perception is a high price.
Rolex, Rolls-Royce, Montblanc, Chivas Regal, Jack Daniels are high priced.
High price is a benefit to their clients too.

The wealthy buy and publicly consume high end products or services.
A Rolls-Royce is bought so people notice it.
If a Rolls-Royce looked very similar to a Ford, would it be as desirable?

Imagine someone in a restaurant has just ordered a $120 bottle of wine.
Would they want to know they can buy a $25 bottle that tastes just as good?
Would they be interested even if they thought that was actually so?

If you want to promote a quality image course you need a high price.
That is considerably higher than otherwise similar courses by other teachers.

Decide what to add to your brand (your courses) to justify higher price.
Rolex made its watches bigger and heavier with a unique wrist band.
Callaway golf clubs made its drivers oversized.
Montblanc pens are fatter/
Chivas Regal Scotch whiskey ages longer (12 years not 8).

What are you going to do to build a quality image for your courses?

Narrow the focus.

Consider a better name (like film stars but for your course or school).

Maybe add something distinctive and then sell at a higher price.

5. Are you really teaching art?

Art is an opportunity for students to unwind and play with materials.
They are only limited by their physical abilities and imaginations.
In other words art is therapeutic.
This indicates the expressive component of art.

But that is only one part.
For even with the very youngest child, there is a discipline.
This discipline is more profound and exacting than mere play.

Art provides a chance for achievement of the less intelligent too.
This apparent quality, pin-points the non-verbal characteristic of art.
Language is just not a necessary condition for art to exist.
It may in fact be an indictment of our methods for assessing intelligence.
There is an excessive emphasis on a child's language abilities (even in art).

Art should be intelligent use of natural expressive abilities.
This intelligent employment is the creative aspect of art.
The thoughts may come before or during the work with the materials.
Then all energy is applied to the task of realizing the idea in the media used.
Pre-determined results have little personal meaning in this context.
They are no substitute for personal choice and involvement.

The infinite range of expressive possibilities will always be limited.
Limits are materials and tools available, as well as the environment.
As a work takes shape, this influences the artist as an additional experience.
Thus art itself is an experience for its creator.
An artist's past experience and the materials are translated into a visual form.

The motivation for the creative act is thus the need for expression.
The method used is be to employ creative thinking to satisfy that need.

Art is creativity expressed using visual material.

Art is a process, or series of processes, where a person responds in action to intrinsically perceived problem stimuli.

This process is potentially endless, as new problem stimuli may be perceived during its course, or at a later date.

They may also be seen as inherent in the medium.

The medium is necessarily visual, although it is not necessarily concrete, nor permanent.

At some stage there is a visual form.

This is subject to change but possesses the properties of the medium.

6. Is art is an intellectual activity?

It's a way of solving problems that you set for yourself.
By using whatever medium is chosen, to work through the problem.
But as the problem is worked out, new problems usually evolve.

The problems are personal and aren't necessarily relevant to others.
The working out is where the visual material create symbols for thoughts.
That is the creative process and the behavior exhibited is creativity.
You are like everyone else but the problems that interest you are different.

But creativity is not limited to art for it's a basic human behaviour.
It's a behaviour used to solve problems if there is no single correct solution.
Just a range of choices from which we must choose before anything is done.
Once a choice is made then the previous choices are no longer available.
They are possible in a modified form, and new choices now appear as well.
This process is the one we all use to navigate our way through life.

So my trust is in logic, the logic of the creative process.
This is my guide and my teaching methods are based on this philosophy.
I pose problems
Each student develops their own solution to the problem they perceive.
I assist a pupil move to more complex problems from a simple starting point.

What is a problem?
A thought for which the individual has no readily available behaviour.

A solution may be attempted (a problem could be avoided or ignored).
A new solution, used before in another context, or blend of several solutions.
Then it is likely this behaviour is creativity.

Creativity is a specific expressive response to perceived problems.
The responses are in the form of concepts (ideas).
They attempt to clarify possible solutions to the problem.
The action (creativity) tests these concepts.

There are mental abilities related to the creative process.
They are in the categories of divergent, convergent and evaluative thinking.
These are identified by many psychologists.

Creativity involves the affective (emotional) and cognitive (thinking).
In art the concepts are seen as an arrangement of visual symbols.
Visual symbols show an artist's understanding of a problem, in visual terms.
Symbols expressed in other ways are language, music or movement.

Creativity provides the structure for the discipline Art Education.
It is a behaviour that is intrinsic to both art and education.
Thus creativity provides the basic conceptual structure for art teaching.
Art education is clarified and understood in its essential simplicity.

Because creativity is behaviour it's like all other behaviours.
It can be developed as a skill.

7. Is there really skilled creativity?

Any behaviour can become more skilled.
Because creativity is a behaviour then skill can be developed.
People considered creative possess that skill.

The two requirements to develop any skill are time and practice.
Performance of a task is related to practice at that task.
With more practice comes control and we can predict what might happen.
Our past experience lets us do this.

As we practice more we become more effective, and results are better.
Because we avoid those things that lead to mistakes and unwanted results.
Our practice has made us efficient.

Most creative people work like this as a result of years of experience.
It seems like magic to the observer but developing skill takes a lot of time.
This is obvious when observing children learn to solve problems.
In the beginning they all do it.
That's how they learn to talk, walk and the other things we take for granted.
Adults learning the same things tend to be impatient.

It is easy to get the confidence necessary for creativity skill to develop.
The thinker needs many problems over a lengthy period of time.
They need to be the kind of problem that generates creativity as a response.

Small increments of additional difficulty are applied at regular intervals.
Eventually a student has sufficient self-confidence to tackle difficult problems.
Problems that would have been impossible at the beginning of this process.

Skills are practiced behaviours.
For skill development there must be an appropriate structure.
Otherwise there will be inappropriate learning.
Best is many repetitions allied to small increases in difficulty.
For creativity many small experiments will beat a major task every time.

Do you develop creativity skill in your students?
Many repetitions with small increments of difficulty are necessary.
But maintaining enthusiasm over a lengthy period of time is also necessary.
How can you make the problems more difficult?

To follow that path refer to my series of books on Coaching Creativity Skill.
They start with Display Art.
This developed from actual courses run by teachers in the 1970's.

8. What is the nature of development?

It is logically impossible to start a process at its conclusion.
For this is only possible if the end-point has already been reached.
Thus it cannot be a valid conclusion, or objective.

Usually a process has an end-point.
So the commencement of the process must not be that end-point.
The movement from the starting point is in the direction of any end-point.
This movement is the notion of development.

This applies particularly to moving to something considered valuable.
Development is the direction of growth towards something of value.
The value is thought to result from the means for the development.
Progression is another term for development.

What if conditions are not desirable for development of a certain kind?
Then the conditions can be modified to be more favourable and appropriate.
This is the role of a teacher.

Development can be a movement towards an ideal behaviour.
Creativity is this kind of behaviour.
Development takes place as an individual finds and accepts limits imposed.
With improved understanding of limits factors, a person works harmoniously.
Balance of the external limits and internal freedom of thoughts and emotions.
The balance becomes self-discipline.
It is achieved by the responsible exercise of freedom within limits.
But there also is a growing breadth of the limiting factors.

Development involves changes of an irreversible nature over time.
Something that can return to its original state hasn't developed.

A teacher's role is to guide the development of their students.

9. How is that related to education?

Education has little agreement about its purpose.
It has probably been determined by the changing needs of society.
Rather than any real concern for the welfare of pupils.
It may not be possible to separate the pupil from society.
But a harmonious development of an individual may be a fruitful approach.

A particular difficulty concerns the rapid accumulation of knowledge.
How is a reduced percentage selected from a growing total content?
Should the nature of the growing content be altered - even drastically?
Can new teaching methods introduce more content in the same or less time?
Change is integral to living in to-day's society, so where does this fit?

In the past, life didn't change much in a generation.
Static goals and unchanging concepts were a basis for education.
This may no longer be feasible?

The wrong objectives may be self-destructive.
There is doubt whether our society can survive unless changes are made.
Society, more than individual members does not seem able to adapt readily.
To fit new and changing circumstances.

The most important educational goal may be learning how to change.
Learning how to adapt to new situations every day is required.
Learning how to learn is now more important than learning how to remember.
It is the learner whose capacity for change, that needs to be developed.
Education should be about helping an individual move in those directions.
The way is nurture an individual's capacity for creative thinking and creativity.

Then education is a process where an individual develops as a person.
Development is the direction of values desirable for an individual and society.
An educated person is one who has (more or less) these desirable qualities.
They have been exposed to processes by which these qualities develop.
The idea of desirable qualities includes breadth and depth of understanding.

Breadth of understanding is required for perceiving alternatives.
Breadth can determine alternatives to enable discriminations to be made.
As such it is justified as an educational activity.
These may be choices, but not necessarily.
Knowledge of alternatives is logically necessary for exercising choices.
It is impossible to choose between alternatives one doesn't know about.
The alternatives are brought into a condition of awareness by another agent.

A teacher is such an agent.
Presentation of alternatives is necessary to develop depth of understanding.
Depth of understanding involves making a decision between alternatives.
Depth is experience with a particular alternative.
Whether or not it was perceived as alternative.

Education is a process of making choices, thus obtaining experience.
This process allows us to make more intrinsically fruitful choices.
It is an on-going process which has infinite possibilities.

The values associated with education may need to be learnt.
But they do not necessarily need to be taught.

Education is a process whereby an individual develops as a person.
This development is attained through experience.
In the direction of values considered ideal for both an individual and society.
The values consist of the various qualities attributed to an educated person.

These values may change from time to time.
They may even be challenged by other previously unconsidered values.
The values don't have equal rank, some are more highly prized than others.
A person is educated in relation to the sum of these qualities acquired.
A person may possess many of the values or a few highly ranked values.
Either way they are considered an educated person.

In our society creativity is a value attributed to an educated person.
This value is highly ranked, both by society and individuals.

10. The nature of art education

Art education is NOT the same as art.
Art education is art in an educational context.
It is art for educational purposes.
Art education must be justified educationally.

Thus art education is only a part of that which is art.
Similarly art education is not the sum of all that is educational.
There's justification for other areas in the rest of the educational spectrum.
These subjects will be differently educational in their objectives.
There may be overlapping of some aspects of one with aspects of another.
But this still doesn't make the two the same.

Art in an elementary school is somewhat different from a high school.
It will certainly different from art in a tertiary level institution.
The former levels have the development of the child as a prime concern.
This might apply to the latter level, there could be vocational objectives.
The student is learning how to become an artist for example.

If it is believed that the business of art in education is to educate.
Then educational solutions rather than artistic ones ought to be considered.
Rather than artistic practices, pupil behaviour, derived from an understanding
of the essential nature of art in the light of educational criteria, is paramount.

Behaviour of any kind only occurs during the course of some action.
Art education ought to be primarily concerned with the process (behaviour).
Rather than the production of objects.
The essential behaviour is creativity so should be the focus of art education.

Creativity and its central role in art is important for education.
The role of art education as a medium for creativity education is critical.
Methods of achieving this should be practical, realistic and work for teachers.
It should be possible to provide individual tuition within a typical classroom
So each pupil moves to more independence according to their need.

Possible course aims:
To develop the uniqueness of each pupil.
To develop confident self-actualisation.
To develop self-responsibility and initiative.
To develop creativity and flexibility of thinking.
To develop bodily skills related to movement.

Possible course objectives:
Related to the above Aims are more specific OBJECTIVES.
Here SKILLS, ATTITUDES and CONCEPTS are integrated.
They are developed, so later stages incorporate preceding stages.

An assumption is creativity is a behaviour possessed by all people.
That is even without teaching.
Appropriate educative methods can develop creativity to a high degree.

The value of appropriate behaviour is stressed.
Only then is there an interaction of perception, affect, cognition and action.
In the manner which is the essence of creativity
Skilled creativity can result.

Aesthetic principles are also considered
All aesthetic material is composed of elements.
The aesthetic principles describe ways in which each element is organised.
In art the elements are concerned with visuality, and so are the principles.
In dance the elements deal with bodily movement as do the principles.
The aesthetic principles are concerned with a relationship.
It is of various aspects of an element to the totality of that element.
Within (say) some bodily movement (dance).
The aesthetic principles are thus concepts which concern relationships.
There are many relationships in any bodily movement or visual image.

Harmony is agreement, closeness, similarity, relatedness.
Of parts to one another.
The parts are related by sharing common aspects or similar visual aspects.

Contrast is dissimilar parts within an element.
Discord is extreme contrast.
Major contrast is obvious, minor contrast a small degree of difference.
Variety may be created by using the contrast principle.

Emphasis is vigour or stress on important parts.
Emphasis of an aspect of an element over another is dominance.
Emphasis may come by using contrast, repetition, or majority of area.

Unity is cohesion, integration, standardisation, or singleness.
Unity adds wholeness to a work.
Unity may come from; one aspect dominant, joining aspects into a
combination, enclosing, repetition, or adding one aspect to the rest.

Rhythm: movement of parts, regular measured beat, flow, throb, pulse.
Rhythm is by repetition, gradation, alteration, radiation or sequence.
Exact repetition may lead to monotony.
Rhythm is related to direction.
In dance it is actual rather than implied (as in art).

Balance: equilibrium, stability in an arrangement of parts in an element.
Balance mat be symmetric (about an axis), or asymmetric (informal).
Balance may be actual or implied.

Proportion is the quantity, or share, of parts within an element.
Proportion is a comparison of parts which may be dominant (most) or
subsidiary (lesser).

11. What does a teaching license allow?

What is a teaching license?
A teaching license provides permission to teach courses.
For a small fee it might be possible to buy a teaching license

Start small.
Do not have many students (maybe 5).
Do not be ambitious in what you will cover.
Do not charge a high fee.
The main aim is to get started and learn what happens.

Target anyone to start with.
Down the track you might specialize in artists but it might not be necessary.

Your second course should build on the first one.
Fix anything that you were unhappy with.
Still keep the course small and cheap.

As you run more courses slowly build the number of students.
Gradually increase the fee charged as you get better.

Once you are confident with your course.
Then consider adding another course with a different focus.
Early students can return to this one.
Eventually you might have a series of courses.

WHERE NEXT:

BUT being a professional artist is NOW harder than it ever was.
These books are on earning money from a professional art career.

GALLEY CO-OPERATION Take the plunge.
http://www.amazon.com/dp/B087637FFW

SELLING STRATEGIES helps people buy.
http://www.amazon.com/dp/B0882JH3WN

MAKE EXHIBITIONS WORK then set up a sell-out!
http://www.amazon.com/dp/B0882MFPGX

ART HIRING beats selling!
http://www.amazon.com/dp/B0884JWR2S

COURSES AND WORKSHOPS and teaching earns money!
http://www.amazon.com/dp/B0884B51JB

AGENTS help productivity.
http://www.amazon.com/dp/B08847Y9KS

YOUR WEBSITE gets referrals.
http://www.amazon.com/dp/B08846SWQP

SELLING PRINTS continuously.
http://www.amazon.com/dp/B08846SWQW

RETIREMENT an early plan best result.
http://www.amazon.com/dp/B0884D9TBP

COPYRIGHT is easy money.
http://www.amazon.com/dp/B0892HWYTV

BUT being a professional artist is NOW harder than it ever was.
This book is the last of a series on earning real money.
From a professional art career.

OPEN A GALLERY and take the plunge.
Open a Gallery - hardback
http://www.amazon.com/dp/B0874JF964

NOT NOW:

Perhaps one of these books could interest you then?

What about your own memories?
YOU could publish them – like I did!
http://www.amazon.com/dp/B087DWKPTP

A simple way to start developing creativity.
If you are a parent, teacher or someone who meets a group regularly?
http://www.amazon.com/dp/B088T1KFQZ

The way most people start to become an artist!
http://www.amazon.com/dp/B088Y1DPL6

About some more of my memories.
http://www.amazon.com/dp/B088Y4RPL9

SEND TO:

Know anyone interested in chocolate recipes? Send them a link then.

http://www.amazon.com/dp/B0882HK9Q9

Know anyone interested in THIS book?

http://www.amazon.com/dp/B08849FV59

www.ingramcontent.com/pod-product-compliance
Lightning Source LLC
Chambersburg PA
CBHW020556220526
45463CB00006B/2327